LIFE OF TOUCHING MOUTHS

Poetry: ". . . it survives
A way of happening, a mouth."

W.H. Auden, *Elegy for W.B. Yeats*

for Cynthia my daughter

Contemporaries

LIFE OF TOUCHING MOUTHS

Vinnie-Marie D'Ambrosio

New York University Press
New York 1971

TABLE OF CONTENTS

MY MOTHER WAS BORN IN AN EARTHQUAKE

My thinboned mothergirl
beneath an olive tree
dreams at an edge
of the Ionian Sea—

how the flat green stone
with its still curves
cools Calabria
and shines against the Greek isles.

Honeyhaired girl
plucking
at the spare grass
beneath the olive tree,

do you never wonder
that Grandma bore you
during the Great Earth-
quake of '08
and that Jove
god of thunder
(philandering neighbor)
snorted and cracked
like a mammoth father
across the water?

Mother, to you
jealous Juno
isn't palpable
on that wind coming in
from Mt. Olympus.

No, Lucetta,
your home saint
is self-blinded Lucia
who carries her eyes
on a china plate

and what *you* feel on the wind
is a light, four-touch
sign of the cross
and the gently meeting
amen of palms.

THE GRAND COMMANDER, 1916
(to my grandfather, 1865-1960)

In coat of red and gold
he duelled, grandpa
versus the two deserters,
under the shadow of the Alps,
lemon-ices sluicing down
the peaks.
Oh it was no grand opera.
That was no pop gun
that got them at dawn
against the grainy gray wall.
Ashen the cat
that shrank at the bang.

GARDEN HANGUP

In Nonno's garden
near some kohlrabi spokes
and sweet william fringes

           a green and yellow contraption stood

like a pavilion
like a swinging car
from a seaside ferris wheel

           all slatted and striped and shaded.

      Six cousins could
      sit and swing in it—
      and come out
      reeling and sick from it.

Usually Nonno
suggested that *strega*
would straighten things out
better than Bromo,
but our stubborn mamas
stirred up Bromo
and clamored,

        "Why on earth did you swing so long?"

      In the dining-room window
      loomed Nonno's garden—
      a househigh tide
      about to crash breakers
      of foamy sweet william.

        "We dunno," we said swaying, gulping

      the soft
      explosion. . . .

SUNDAY WAS ONCE AN INFINITE DAY

I. *Early Morning*

A BELL,
and bells *con brio*
break my Sunday into blessings,
shave it into thousand-pitch,
and plunging chips of fugue
echo and drone
in spongy tones.

But I am taut
for the clear cube-root—
hear it!
buried deep
beneath the soft heap,
alive, alone,
that first
CLANG
hangs,
shines.

II. *After Church*

The fireworks are dazzling!
Under a linden
a trinity of ladies
is aging on a bench
and flapping lips in rapid gossip.
See their gold teeth
shiver in the sun
and how gleams flare like ladders
and pierce the white branches.
Their chatter, crossing wildly,
etches in the flaming air
a dragon's tic tac toe.
(Oh, I'm inclined to be transported
in the cage of fire
to the softdrooping tree.)

III. *Glorious Noon*

Ah, shattered air flakes into pebbles by the bells,
and the pavement is a stretch of sunny breadcrumbs.
If two toasters work ten noondays
in a moment my eyes will flash
bright as a sparrow's.

IV. *Lazy Afternoon*

Never did hoard Sunday in my gullet
nor measured Mediterranean for flight.

V. *Evening*

We never measured on Sundays.
In our house
indefinite recipes
spun down
my mother's brain
and ancient platters
linked
in lines of infinite
aunts,
and in the kitchen, grandmother's hands were scooped
moons
where even the blackest
mushrooms
would light up full
and spill
forward.
She poured from her crescents
numberless rhythms:
flour (flying),
pepper seeds
(wet).

VI. *Midnight*

Sunday was a sainted corpse,
eternal and perfumed—
and suddenly assumed!
And every week it took a ride
as I turned over on my side.

THE BIG INDIAN NUT FESTIVAL

Sandy got wind of the Indian nuts,
and this is how he made his raid:
sneaked one brown pearl
out of the dish,
then leaped from Pa's
mohair chair, to the tipping rocker,
to the red and white wicker,
bridgelamp-poles quaking,
their bonnets shaking,
and Sandy breaking out the kernel!
He was no squirrel,
just a *great mutt*
who knew how
to celebrate.

KISS

The room is tall.
To its dark brain
I raise my arms
and pierce night's ears
with a kiss.
Father's shadow
is on my wall
along with the falling forsythia.

*

Then through the venetian blinds
the sun publishes kisses.
And we tap the day's divisions
and punctuate noon
and mother and classes
with kisses.

*

Those are cousins all amok,
frenzying the streets!
Goodbye! Hello!
Life of touching mouths.

*

Soon
very soon
a dim kiss breathes.
In country town.
I stroke his eyes.
His moonwhitened lids.

FINAL SEPTEMBER

I. *The Last Twenty-Five Pound Ice of Summer*

September's wind revved up,
as all along our road a line of loose light hedges
turned silver.
The black elderberries
and sumacs arched back,
and I looked for my brother at the road's end
in the narrow sky.

There came the wagon-blaze!
Bucking on the hilltop
the cake of ice
sparkling
radiating rapid beams
and hot broken lights—

a living diamond
it seemed
an alchemist's stone
my brother had dug
from a thundrous athanor
deep in Terry Hill

to haul to our porch
to make storms in the ice-box
and influence by its flashings
our last lumps of butter and
the one small bottle
of country milk.

I watched my brother
and his wagon's leaping gift:
something said at summer's leaving
we'd be sitting to sip
an Egyptian wine
and a creamy Greek cheese
from the cabalistic crocks
in the ice-box.

II. *The Miracle: My Brother Teaches Me to Dive*

He sought
to initiate me,
and knelt behind me.

My arms shaking,
stringing towards the dark yellow-wool hills,
neck a dead spring,
shanks shivering,
and toes clinging in the darkening air
to the wooden rung of the wooden dock,
I prayed.
He grasped my ankles,
held still,
and then the flashing
overturn.

I yielded
on the cold edge.

*

Ah, who knew the water would be velvet and warm?
Where was the line between body
and water?
I bobbed, and a thin freezing boundary
moved. From my chin
down
I was the lake.
I bobbed: from my shoulders down
I was the lake.
I ducked, and raised my arm:
I was the lake, but for my trembling lunatic arm.
I floated—and the crown of my head was the lake,
my exposed face was that purple-red racing sky,
those wild and icy
black-brown hills;
the rest of me
was the still, warm
water.

III.   *Fat Skunk's Fadeout*

Fat skunk walking into MGM sunset,
waddling up the middle of our road,
you are fakely brave,
old uncle skunk;
the summermen are all smoked out
of their dim bunks
and the kids are all honed
from Labor Day
and you've no call to waddle blackly
nonchalant, languid and leonine,
wiggling your middle white stripe;
fuzzy filmstrip, at The End you'll be merely
wrapped around the reel of our road.

INTO MEMORY

(For Dorothy Johnson Fulmer, who died in a fire
while trying unsuccessfully to save two of her sons.)

Beneath ancient trees of my Indian streets
we walked
was it a thousand times?
Far beneath trees
towards school rooms
ambling,
soft sunny needles falling on your face,
our skin-gloved hand
bones mixed and curling,
you hummed, talked,
explicated,
wildly blonde
at the side of this dark
murmuring
introversion.

Ducks like blue mushrooms storm
up from the grass,
snap at our shoes
and we hop a sharp circle.
Never mind!

Swinging sandwiches,
we breathed those mornings
the long connections of close-hushed night,
shaping air like clay
in codes
and songs.
The beautiful boy we madly loved,
that insinuating
Aztec
from a southern heaven,
he had sent to each
one butterfly wing.

On mine—*tu eres la luna...*,
for you—*tu eres el sol....*
The joy! we laugh rejoining the wings,
and the binary secret
unfolds thin pleats in bubbles of sunlight
and flies up to the spartan trees.

Glassy leaves tinkle
in the cowlicks of trees
and we hear some seagulls
cry in the marshes, and
soft sounds of trains
bearing
us and our books,
was it a thousand times?

I knew you all
the chrysalis years.

Where you flourished I loved too,
in Grandmother Whitman's tight dim house.
I smell her nurture, her chicory salad
alive with lemon,
the smokerimmed crocks
of syrups and light pink beans.
Rising in the corner
the giltpocked moon
tolls the unrolling afternoon,
and blackwood chests
burst
waxlighted roses;
patinas flash
again and again as shadows
shiver around the rooms.
Carpets and lace
were your cocoon.

But how freely you grew!
Action burst out from your thought
natural as a kindled breath.
Jailers could not clip you!
The night they caged you, my
television (that bloated frog)
blinked at your glowing
principles,
and typists clacked about you
like katydids.

Long before that night,
on one sparkling lake-morning,
tan and careful and barefoot we filed
into my summer-town's cemetery.
The bees, like hovering nails,
buzzed
as you fell on a concrete cross.
"Snap me!"
Actress! Feigning agony!
A dozen phrases were in your body
as rays of sunlight licked the film
with that dancing crucifixion.

The gestures of your mind were honed
in Ibsen, Shaw and Wilder.
Your life was one full action.

I knew you knew our difference
and that it was no hindrance.
Lying on the lakeside lawn, drying
in the evening sun—
how bushy-red
the sumac fence—
we played a mystic game, Essence.

"Oh he is this and she is that"
and I you say am
"a Persian rug"
and surprised they all shout Bravo! Good!
Your words caressed, you loved me well
though I still drowsed in passive dreams.

In the shining gymnasium
on the final school day
we are offered stiff faces encased in a book,
a hundred scrawled wishes, all the same.
Near your smile, with shaking pen,
no vale-te,
no girl's farewell,
just the sigh,
you write
"Oh, Vinnie."

Oh, Dorothy.

Some few months since
we feasted here with a dozen friends.
Our Aztec sat among us too—
and three memories nodded, smiled.
We chatted, all on velvet chairs,
of race and poetry.
The cunning and intricate
turns of the talk
could not
with their tendrils
cover the gleam
of the bright blonde wine.
Beneath the vine of chatter
these clusters of behavior
explode
in me:

only your voice ringing lines,
Ginsberg, Corso, made better than they are—
the table stunned;
only you and Chet
telling how
with shepherd's crook
you took in
a fourth son
who was richly colored. . . .

Indians taut and silent,
greenhaired guards, do you shield the dirt road
where she shone, she shone?

Like a carousel of days
chance has spiralled around the darling
plucking rings of merry light.
Dizzied chance, how astonished
to catch at last
on twirling fingers
all those golden rings of light.

ALLA MORA

O you Sibyl

omenless
broken from the egg of Rome

copping
syntactic kicks
in ticklish Latin
from Cassell's Big One
(with its thumb index)
and flipping the golden M with your thumb,

ab ovo, Sibyl:

> "*Micare digitis*: To play
> a game
> which involved
> holding out of the fingers
> suddenly
> for another to guess
> their number.
> (Cf. the Italian game
> of *alla mora*.)"

So the verb means vibrate, flicker, glitter.
And the idiom with *digitis*
sketches a picture
of flickering,
glittering,
shining
fingers!

*

In Rome
their togas swirl
their clenched fists fly
to circle-center
the fists burst there
the men shout
a sudden sneeze
of synchronized numbers
and that spasm spit
in day-to-day Latin.

How I remember *alla mora*—
my six uncles and happy father
fresh-banished
to the garden-touching basement.
Fierce in guesswork
they join a circle
(I crouch)
a growling circle
(I wait)
and explosive,

DIEci!
UNo!
OTto!
NOve!
(and more and more!)

The united cry chops me
but the tail syllables soothe
so masculinely murmured

and a royal blue sky
glasses the windows

and wives upstairs
sit serene above the glitter

of Roman candles in the cellar . . . . .
Sibyl, you hear that ancient roar.

SNARES

I.

In northern Vermont
because the breeze was fair
I sprayed my hair
with a sweet-holding lacquer.
Urban error!
I undid the id
of a Hyde-like bee
and wildly he rushed
into the brunette bush
and sang of tropic ecstasy
below my left earlobe.

Nestling in the floral dark
he thought the south had come to him.

II.

The Van Gogh show
when I was young
was going wild.
Reds, greens
eclipsed numberless
dreaming guards,
and spirit-golds
rivered around me
all in streams.
I was so swathed
in this lightribboned mass
that I dared to cross the law
and touched with one tremble
the violent forbidden
consenting canvas.

Yielding,
wrapped in a shroud
of a thousand shreds,
I veered on a fantastic death. . . .

STEEPLE CHASE AT THOMPSONVILLE

Through green-
breathing fields
in Thompsonville
David and I strolled.
And
ran a
mental
race.

Our aim, to seem
more ornamental.

"Elm!" Pointing.
"Birch!" Circling.
"Willow!" Stopping.

Kissing.
Beneath elms and birches
and wild wet willows.

Each
secretly
sprinting.

"Butter-and-eggs!" Plucking.
"Clover!" Treading.
"Day-lily!" Stroking
the silky orange
edges.

And thus love begins, ambling and
crashing over sighing fields.

POEM TO NIGHT'S LANDSCAPE

Your lips will influence
these blown flowers
back into budhood.

And your silver moon nail
will ascend
and fall.

And the pale apricot
tipping the branch
will bend up
to gentle teeth.

GAZE

(to E.V.)

What brown are your eyes,
these sweet polished chestnuts?
Are they the dimness
in my grandmother's house?
The wood of her bed,
her shadowy primness and russet lace?
The hermit piano in the corner
with its shell drawn tight?
The dark coffee vortices
swirling hollow cells?
No twilight wine swims brown as your gaze.
My mind rolls down hills like a hoop in a wind.

OPUS

(to A.P.)

I thought one day we'd
build a mound
of scarlet leaves
ten horses high

like a merry church

and near it plant
a window-glass
filled with faces
of sharon-roses

back of which
on autumn mornings
I'd till an oven
for mushrooming
loaves
or prune a summer
chifferobe
or irrigate
the works
of an English clock

and you'd warm a cloud
of sheep with crumbs
scooped
from apples
or comb a bush
of early snow
for syrup
and arias of cardinals:

the mass—
red flowers red fruit red sugar red song—
has focused so long
in this burning-glass.

WHEN IN A SMALL AGONY

When in a small agony
at two-thirty or three
you whisper a cry
that is a small woodland thing
and for an instant we wonder why
(the cry a flash
puzzling the cool air)
and you salve the agony
with a burrowing, hurried,
I want to whisper
consolation
far into your ear's tunnel
but it swallows my breath,
sheets of wildflowers
bend in whistling caves
and my thought is a humming bird
a whirring
hardly visible blur
fading into owl's eyes.

GREEN ACANTHUS

Green acanthus
curled its fronds
near fluted trees

and under easy gods
squadrons of birds
tilted rainbows

and fish
flicked like candles
and boiled up airy awnings

and animals
blushed untempted

and Adam wore
the sweet shade
like a purple cloak.

    *

Too soon a gray dawn when he frenziedly bended
and clenched and crazed and petered and yawned

small rodent yawns around white china teeth.
Nervehoard dimming, he schemed

like a numb squirrel about to pluck, bored,
synaptic acorns. Then slunk away from acorns.

Strummed an abacus. Torpidity recurred.
Afternoons, pokereeno in penny arcades.

Never once demurred of the softening brawn.
By eve was an amnesiac, mincing.

FANTASY OF THE DIVORCED LADY

I. *Do All Men Hate Highboys? She Asked Pathetically*

The chest,
dark mass
at the foot of their bed,
sprouts at four points:
pineapples poised,
gleaming bow-knees.

Their paralyzed pillows
have eyes that fly open
in the night sometimes,
and the volume balloons—

mahogany gorilla
with twenty brass nipples.
Sometimes at dawn
it is spider inverted,
its interior spinning
wild gauze webs
of garters, beads
and magical gowns.

"What is it? Godawful,"
husband said,
and withdrew from deposit
his pleated shirts
like paper aeroplanes.

The Peruvian pilot
(late of Lima)
drawled some scents:
fruitpulp
minty wool
hair tonic.

Lemonbalm on his hands.

Her two palms
were but lambs
in his hands.

Muffled his eyes,
dim moles from a leopard
peeled in a jungle.

But limbs correctly
angled.

How large the fact loomed:
he wished to lie,
and soon.

She slowly spooned her melon.
He drained his yellow drink.

III.   *Jerome's Letter to Innocent I, Fourth Century*

Dear Innocent:

Returned from my journey. I now set forth
an account of a case I saw in the north.
in the north.

Confined by old grudge
in noon's scalding jail
a frenzied youth lied
for a panful of dew
and love-sin confessed
(torture making haste).

Thus, dear Innocent,
falsely convicted
a Ligurian wife
was stretched on the mountain
on adultress's rack;
her feet were set fire,
red daisies in the heat;
her breast brightly ribboned
by honeygold blood.
Vapors of peaches
arose to her chant:

"O better to whirl
into life everlasting
than—lying—die
interiorly."

Ere slaying the youth,
they slaked his thirst.
His black mouth moaned the truth,
but the wife had died first.

The husband (sorrowful!)
gnashed his teeth and burst his skull.

Holy Vicar, unblamed your post.
We revere our martyrs most.

Jerome.
(At home.)

MOON AS MEDUSA

Such easy, easy hours
when their porch has started fading
into a long and dark and middle gulf—

his mouth and mine brushing and rubbing
and freshening
and parting, O's joining and
dropping
and swelling small and
adhering and brushing
in long and easy creations: those mouth rounds and
ovals, those slow brims arching,
the mouth-curves like four acrobats
in a drowsing circus
bending over and over, partners
of touching-shapes—pears, hearts, wreathes—
until at once only one flesh-ring lives,
a lamp of lips,
a knowing dayglow valve;

and our legs and arms and torsos
are undressed
furniture,
distant,
like the mattress's abysses and
the flimsying rugs and the pulverizing
soundless windows;

as if all—bedroom and body-extensions—
have begged to be excused,
and thinned down,
and gone outside to the elm, itself
perforating into night,
or farther out to the moon's flying wane,
or vanished over the skies' aisles:

all in a passion of exit
so low-keyed and un-insistent
that the lips never notice in the
lit concentration
on their own easy hours;

but always something (it was
the moon once when
clouds like snakes' mouths
were falling around her mowing jaw)
some Medusa-fury
fires the edge of the elm
and then the grainy window,
and under the shower of light
the lips' shadows
dance a
turnabout
in the thickening room.

IN A CARIBBEAN CONVENT GARDEN

Today
I am the unwishing
and sinless
flower of Yumurí.

*

I am the greenlashed eye
of my fishshaped isle.

*

There is rune-dew
on me.

*

I grow near a grave
but I move and drowse and move.
I marvel that
I am the bee's blue dream.

*

I forgive the monk
who passes me
beakdeep in book
who thinks
unthinking of my musk.

*

A bee above me stalls, I am glad
as his feet press
into the pistil
of a fullblown
mothcurved cloud.

*

I never blush.

*

I am sleepy
with science.

THE MEXICAN DAREDEVIL

He strode hard at the bar
and barked ¡QUE TAL!
and clamped his arm
on friend's wingbone!
Lucky vise! Fierce muscleband!
Jaunty!

I'm sorry I lack
that starchy surface.
I unroll my embrace
like a scarf.

AFTERNOON VISIT TO AN OLD VIOLINIST

The first violinist (retired)
of the Mexican National Symphony
sliced
an avocado.

The sun boxed in
the kitchen table.
Dust-ribbons
whitened the air.

*"¿Entonces, vendiste
tus violinos, viejo?"*

Tick and tock
of a hot cricket.

At the heart of the sunbox
the velvet avocado
(strange green fiddle)
and old-man's hands.

Still afternoon.
The birds dozed
in kitchen cages.
The dog snored
sotto voce.

CURED IN MEZOAMERICA

Restored
at last!

by a twelve-cent
dish
of orangecolor
soup
and its drained
core
etched and sweet —
a fillet of fish.

Where gutknives
gored
moments ago
now lights
glow

and the sky and clouds
take on
their old look
like cow-cream
raddling a blue glass tray.

And with my friend, 72
flown in from Paris
where they stretched and stitched
her face
to an angel's tension—

flitting
above the stonequilted track
we're a smooth couple of
welkin-drops.

MEXICAN GOTHIC

Rivera's mistress
had recently miscarried
so in her shadowed room
she painted a foetus
and hung it like a garish wing
wringing wet on the wall.

Her chromium bed
(that ark of hell)
she painted next
and blazoned its sheets
with a rosy blossom —
her belly;
and she scratched in with clarity
knives lying bloodtipped by
and doctors glaring foully.

The frames she cut
from a tropical tree
were properly stark
and primitive.

Then she said: "Diego,
the house is so gloomy.
While you're at your murals
in town until four
I'm in the doldrums.
Gardening is maddening—
the plants are always
enceintes.
And I've painted a dozen dead babies."

"Off to the fair!" said Diego Rivera,
and the furrows flew
from Frida's brow.

Oleander-poinciana-jacaranda
blooms
filled the court chasm
with the lambent perfumes
of their nightlong orgasm.

And the moon on Frida's roof
in Coyoacán
was uncannily white
that first of November.

But the carnival folk
All Souls' Night
gamboled beneath
kaleidoscopic light—
for dancers in a frenzy
strummed
with tincted plumes
the tin-mandolin
Mexican moon.

Bathed in this
chromatic drama,
all night the two wandered
handing out silver,
bent on buying
a vast population—
of skeletons
skittish
in *papier maché*!

Had a whole town suffered
a gay decimation?

Some of the skeletons
were eight feet long
(nipped in the bud
not a moment too soon).
These fellows had bones
in yellow and green,
skulls and square teeth
of a lurid-red,
large knotty ribs in ultramarine.
Some
     were spined with curly flames,
some
     had wrists like purple plums.
One animated relic
(abnormally pelvic)
groaned papery groans
with piebald bones.

So Diego unfurled
his chamois purse
to make Frida nurse—
to a host of ghosts!

An osteoid lady
was the smallest of their lot:
hair of amethyst,
pink patches on her face, she
was lightly shouldered
by an Indian tot
who lent a queer pathos
to her necroscopic grace.

Indeed, following the Riveras
and bearing the waggish treasures
was a long compliant line
of sleepy slumping hirelings.

On the second of November,
with sunfresh laughter,
Frida and Diego
began their cosmic task.
Unhelped by servants
(who knelt at Mass),
they hung the first skeleton
from a kitchen rafter.
Another linked chap
they looped near a bed,
and cheered the gloomy house
with all their dangling dead.

Diego, the good man,
knew the tonic for her fear:
he must hint that while he lived
he was Death's puppeteer.

Well, phthisic Frida died and now she is *cum deo*.
The house, you know, became a national *Museo*.
To this day it's crammed
with the saved and the damned.

THE NEW NAME

*(The Nethermead, the Vale of
Cashmere and the Rose Garden
are located in Prospect Park.)*

I never really saw you in the Nethermead
frizzling yourself, snake,
scalloping your grass,
but I know your bunching-up ways.

You don't sing your song out.

You're a winding bas-relief,
you're a love attack,

and on this green and white morning
I have the feeling
that your trailing alley
is slowly braiding
a new name for me.

***

As a bride I shocked a silver rat
who fled crashing on the cobblestones
in the Vale of Cashmere.
Air like gray moss
choked the Vale
while his mean toes scraped up
a dictionary
of deathy dust,
not new-name dust, not
the sweet glinting pollens
my breath sucks for now.
I was far
from astounded
and warned a few children.

***

This tree rising formal
at the end of the Rose Garden,
it's large, it's dark!
It has so sighing a symmetry
I must look all morning along
at it—and by noon
dip a spiral branch
in the pool at its roots,
curving the name, curving
the verdant name. . . .

CYNTHIA IS COMING IN ON THE NIGHT FLIGHT

My eyes'
stiff
linear
lightrays
scrape the sky's dark acres
and finally like
chopsticks
delicately grasp
the big Brazilian airliner
within two tips
and guide it (touch and go)
towards
this airport's
moist lips.

JULY NIGHT (to a child of divorce).

It was under a country willow
counting out
night's constellations
that I heard a stranger's
child crying.
A pure cry,
it spread,
rippling warm grasses
like a lyrical wrist,
fanning the Dragon
with an infant's old phonology;
and then it fell
in rushes, swelling,
until all the sobbing air
was luscious.

At long last, it
erased its own mouth
and rested me
vastly.

But then I was parched
for my sweet known-crying:
my talling child,
my spartan,
has spilled no tear
this year,

and I found myself raging
to the freshened stars,
calling them
to glisten
in her eyes.

IF I WERE A MAKER I'D

make a melon
        orange in yellow
add a rod
fret it   and string it

and trim a pick
from a suppleplump pit.

My tools would burgeon
bunches of grapes and

then ghosts in motley
no-shaped and graced
would pin the grapes

to their pointed shoes   and ring-a-ling them.

One shade would dandle my banjo gently—
and soon

you'd see a melon roll through air!
you'd see grapes leaping and lighting!

and you'd hear my mooncurled song!

THE COLTUNS AND THE GANGSTER

Bea Coltun's baby
was carried to the woods
by an Italian gangster
who kissed and cooed
and was good
with babies.

Had Bea Coltun known
a *gangster* was beholden
to Baby Robert for renewal
in that green temple,
the two alone and cooing
        (where trees were full
        of Black Hands
        growing
        like eggplants),
she'd have held a revolver
in pale trembling fingers
and taken her baby.

But when they strolled back
from their woodsy ramble,
the Italian gangster
bubbling over, tickling baby,
she thought,
Those Italians,
what warm souls!

Then the Coltuns and the gangster
and the rest of the guests
all ambled in
to the Summer Inn.

Inside, the shaman
(that is, the gangster)
and his famished council
wolfed down bowls
of holy lasagna.
Their souls, seeming leavened
by ritual *al dente*,
basked in the Coltuns

who were nibbling at their pasta
radiantly.

THE GRACE OF CYNTHIA'S MAIDENHOOD

He chants a boy-chant,
a whisper-chain
:   I heard that you heard that I said that I

love

you
and a silverbird hovers,

shades the blush on her face,
the paling mouth;

and into her eyes
fall the shining feathers
of shyness and pleasure.

THE STORE AT THE BACK OF HER GARDEN

Green vines
like lakewaves in summer
whisper in breadth
rustle in height
on three storeys
of scarred brick
at her garden's southern edge.
Lights seem to whistle on the soft wall
as they ripple
down to her plants
sinking with dusty tomatoes.

She thinks how odd
that years ago
behind the vines
(*profound vines*)
an old man ran a flowershop
like a liontamer.
Bursts
of orchids and elephants' ears
she remembers
stood whipped and chopped and bleeding
in cardboard jugs.
But purple trumpets lie there now
row on row
dark and efflorescent—
mysterious stoppered bottles
filled with deep wines.
Labels
float above the shelves
blossoming in the dimness.
A doberman pinscher
glides through the awning-shaded indoor air
like a water moccasin.

my golden-pupilled crocuses
have caught
with their tackles of desire
a heroic
a silvery fish.

Fragile stranger
pinned to the loam
your shivering edges
folded like fins
and sawing at the wind:
how you glint
in the sun
freed from the candy shop
freed this noon
from the sweet gum
a schoolchild chews.

But why did they snare you
so saltless
a *fruit de mer*?

Can the new blue wind
or the sun's massive tongue
or the waters of the Bay
have engendered in my crocuses
the power to hunt
to hook Aegean flashes
in a shining paper fish?

Shall Juno be neat
and bury it with the trash?

GAMBADO ON AMSTERDAM AVENUE

In the air
in the air
the perfect justice of music and musk
balancing floating.

The city street a Renaissance
garden
a world's fair walkway

with piccolo purls
ravelling out of trees
and a soft saxophone
shoving an aircone
from an unlatticed window.

A girl
arching her arms
to an elm's low branch
like the Bridge of Sighs.

And who am I?

I smell the boulevard
the cornsilk grass
cut into broad
squares.

I sense
this summer Wednesday
wider
than my summer sleeves.

Musicians! have you seen
a storm of warm doubloons?
For the last long hour
sieved from the sun they've bobbed
in the air
below the elm.
I left my eyes
there!
Softly, poets!
they are this morning's
ransom.

I remember
my green chiffon
in its winter closet
as a dungeon light.

But for now—
no toes to step on,
now, the flying
Blindwoman's dance!

A SUDDEN DESIRE TO SEE MY COLLEGE TOWN
IN NEW ENGLAND

My heart is hot for place
as though where I am is not there
and there is where barns are

striped with planks
that alternately slant
letting in air

and I tear those seesaws from the walls
and wrap myself
in bandages of aging wood
to soothe my angry skin

and then I see
what I have done:

under Mount Tom
a barn grins
a gapboned skull
with rustling tobacco palms
browning inside

sweating dry like brains.

IN THE CEMETERY-KEEPER'S LODGE

Bordeaux, France, February
19 (Reuters)—

Angry women tried
today
to lynch
the mother of two chil-
dren who were shot and killed
by their father Monday
after a nine-day
police
siege.

André
Fourquet,
a 38-year old bulldozer
operator,
shot the chil-
dren and then killed
himself as policemen in arm-
ored cars
closed
in around
the house
where he held them at bay.

Throughout the siege,
Fourquet told the police
he would let
the children
go
if his estranged wife
were
brought to him "so
that I can kill her."

About 30 women,
shouting "Let's lynch
her!" and
"It's a scan-
dal—she let them die!"
turned the funeral
of Francis and Aline Fourquet,
11 and 13,
into a near-riot.

They mobbed the mother, Mrs.
Micheline
Berton.
When she broke away
they chased
her around the cemetery.

Finally, she took refuge
in the cemetery-keeper's lodge.
Shouting insults, the women
kicked in a window
and tried
to tear
down railings.

Three truckloads of policemen
escorted Mrs. Berton
from the cemetery.
One of the women was
arrested.

The women apparently
felt
that Mrs. Berton
should have attempted
to plead with Fourquet
for the children's
release

during the siege.
She said
at the time
that
she was convinced
her presence
would only enrage
Fourquet.

CAT LOOKING INTO FISHTANK

he's a gargoyle
with whisker-hooks

he's a
cat
in calico fuzz
rubbing his ribs
against the glassy
apse
pressing his nose
on the rose window

oh yes
his unmewing glare
lies on
crystal squares
oh yes
this cat
fractures colors
somewhat above
the water-altar
but his look
is deep

and he's unquaking
in his quatrefoil

*

the bottleful of parishioners
green from the filtered sun
fastens on the vision
of the grim green cat

hymns
gurgle
heavenward

(A Found-Poem, *New York Times,* 2/20/69)

ON CHRIST'S CURSE AT THE BARREN FIG TREE

I.

Jerusalem's tree
strains to spring figs, too late. Calm
is the day, the dust.

*

Mary hides her hair
in envelopes of blue wool
dread, her dreams rattling.

*

Shrive, or shrivel that
tender green tree? Christ, will you
wither a city?

II.

Snow blazed, so we lashed
rugs to our tree, and ghosts' feet
tramped on unborn figs!

*

I love the crystal
fig-points, but rich careless kings
toss them on stone plates.

*

Figscape on my sill
swollen by moon and mirror:
fruit in holocaust. . . .

FULCRUM AT LAST NIGHT'S P.T.A. MEETING

We are Jews we screamed
remember we are Jews the pinch
of the doorbell
the trains that swam snakelike
remember we are Jews

the dream of death was a cape, the gas
I clipped on at my neck
last night, the dream-hood,
my Jew-hood, the gas
slipped over my hair my eyes my mouth
I gnawed the hood for light for air

Yes yes she once said the priestess to my couch
Dr Smith said yes
you dreamed all your life
you were black and uggily muggily
double dutch in the morning
the shadows rooted ropes
up the thick dark air
you know your life
was a crouching
from a lynching

Amazing!
we hummed and buzzed
we blacks
are getting old and lost
we hummed in beauty

I paid a dollar a minute
for that

Where lemons take easiest wing
from the warm trees
they'll drop! to my palms
the buckets will ring!
with the shining things

I am Jewblack pied
Last night I died
and rose
and piped away my children
crying notes

(on the suicide by hanging of Ilse Koch,
the bitch of Buchenwald)

BALLAD OF THE LAMPS, with instructions
                    to the reader
                    for singing the refrain
                    ad lib

What
could the tattoos
sing,
while filtering their golden
watts?

They sang:

> "Bark skinned
> from forests
> is darkly traced
> and delicate
>
> restless
> rustling
> over shining
> mushrooms
>
> along the woods'
> floor . . ."
> [*Hiss
> obscenities.*]
>
> "We grunted
> our twigs grappling
> in unwilling
> passion

boughs weighted
with lights
like claws
and she watched

mouth
mowing . . ."
[*Hiss
obscenities.*]

They sang:

"The bitch
of the black cave
has turned into
a stalactite

her toes
twitching . . ."
[*Hiss
obscenities.*]

Who knew her—
(God, all refused her!)
the Polish refugee,
caught seven times
in the Jew net?

Old
and fat
and poor.

Halls of applause
rattling
in a patched brain.

At last we met
and I wanted her
inside my door.

She came.
I poured the vermouth
of old sunrises
and said, Borrow my piano
in the mornings, Bluma.

And her arms flew,
and golden raisins
gleamed at the elbow,
and her dying skin
was heaving dough.

Done, shoulders damp,
she'd talk
beneath the parrots and swans
in the Roman garden
painted on my wall.
Wild Schumann huddled

beneath mute feathers,
ghastly parades
of brothers and children
kissed with soft beaks,
and I always said,
Tell me more!

Once the pain pushed
her to draw a line:
It is not fine of you,
she said.
We stared at wine,
and spoke no more of Poland.

In Warsaw's winter, once
she bartered, she the ripe artist
bartered her piano
for a shredding quilt.
My guilt is worse.
I handed her a sieve of hours,
and as return
peered under old leaves
at the haunted bird.

I will go into
the small black room
where my work lies scattered
and the letters on the keys
are trembling fires
and the linoleum
is a rag of ice
under my penitent feet.

But Bluma, those mornings—
how the bright rooms laughed with music
while we wept!